A WORDSWORTH HANDBOOK

MOTORCYCLES

W0008555

Wordsworth Editions

First published in England 1994 by
Wordsworth Editions Ltd
Cumberland House
Crib Street
Ware
Hertfordshire SG12 9ET

ISBN 1–85326–813–5

Right: *Honda's world-renowned Gold Wing*

Previous page: *Moto Guzzi Daytona 1000*

Superlaunch Ltd thank the many manufacturers for their
generous assistance with the production of this book, and
Andrew Wright for additional artworks

Designed and produced by Superlaunch Ltd
P O Box 207, Abingdon, Oxfordshire OX13 6TA, England
Text conversion and pagination by
August Filmsetting, St Helens, England
Colour separation by Seagull Reproductions Ltd, London
Printed and bound in the Czech Republic by Svoboda

CONTENTS

EARLY DAYS

The Daimler Riding Car was the first motorcycle in the world, taking to the streets of Bad Cannstatt, near Stuttgart, on 10 November 1885.

Gottlieb Daimler, the son of a master baker, was born on 17 March 1834, and became first an apprentice gunsmith, then worked as an engineer, before being appointed as the technical manager of Reutlingen Brotherhood, where he was to meet a young draughtsman, Wilhelm Maybach. They went on to form an inseparable team; even when Daimler went independent in 1882, Maybach joined him, and together they developed their ideas, finally fulfilling their dreams when the engine was fitted into a two-wheeler they intended to form the cheapest means of experimentation. In this way, they almost incidentally gave birth to the first motorcycle.

The greenhouse, situated in the park behind the Daimler villa, had been converted to a design office in 1882, and is today a museum. Daimler had worked steadily on the development of a small light engine that would be suitable for universal application, and took out patent DRP 34926 on 3 April 1885, on an engine that had a

Gottlieb Daimler

Wilhelm Maybach

4

Nikolaus August Otto

the vapour is highly compressed

3. A downward stroke, powered by the explosive ignition of the vapour
4. An upward stroke in which the spent gases from the explosion are expelled from the cylinder

Valves in the cylinder head allow the petrol vapour to enter and the exhaust to leave.

It was to be another decade before the motorcycle pioneers in France, in Germany and in England followed Daimler's lead. Meanwhile, Daimler and Maybach had turned their attention to engines for ships and four-wheeled road vehicles.

closed crankcase and a single vertical cylinder and which became jokingly known as the grandfather clock.

This fast-running engine, designed on the principle of internal combustion, was to transform everyday life in the twentieth century, being based on a four-stroke cycle that was developed by Nikolaus August Otto in 1876.

The strokes refer to the movements of a piston within its cylinder.

1. A downward stroke, in which the petrol vapour is drawn into the cylinder
2. An upward stroke, in which

The upright Daimler engine of 1885, known as the 'grandfather clock'

5

DE DION AND OTHER PIONEERS

Daimler 'Riding Car' 1885; the first motorcycle in the world

French pioneers included Comte Albert de Dion, and his partner Georges Bouton, who, like many others, had tried to develop a viable steam-powered bike, finally turning to the internal combustion engine they built on a tricycle in 1895. This was powered by a petrol engine capable of 1,500rpm, virtually double that of Daimler's engine.

A water-cooled, two-cylinder petrol-engined bike was first designed in Germany at about the same time, by Hildebrand and Wolfmüller, while over in England, Colonel Henry Holder had produced a peculiar two-cylinder model which had pistons at both ends of each cylinder and was therefore in fact a four-cylinder engine.

By the end of the nineteenth century, the firm of De Dion Bouton et Cie embarked on the production of engines which were for sale over the counter. It also licensed production in England, Germany, Belgium and the United States. Its engines could fit in a large

Early attempts to site the engine at least were imaginative, and posed the same problem for all of the early manufacturers. Illustrated below are just a few of the more popular experiments, which show that manufacturers were not always convinced that they had originally discovered the answer as, like Singer, they frequently experimented with alternative positions.

1 Singer (see *also* 8)
2 Werner and Enfield
3 Phelon and Moore
4 British Excelsior
5 Hildebrand and Wolfmüller
6 Beeston
7 Ormonde
9 Humber

variety of vehicles, and thus the internal combustion engine was available and even if not always reliable, these engines were snapped up by customers eager to prove that they knew how to design and even manufacture motorcycles.

The variety of early designs and the siting of the engine were manifold, with some engines being mounted above or at the side of the front wheel; others were mounted above or behind the rear wheel, while the problems of connecting one of the wheels to the continuous drive belt proved to be a major stumbling block for many would-be manufacturers.

It was Michel and Eugene Werner, two enthusiastic Russian exiles living in Paris, who after much experimentation introduced in 1901 a bike with the engine located low down in a diamond-shaped frame, situated midway between the two road wheels. The effect was a winner, providing both stability and a much lower centre of gravity for the motorbike.

In 1902, the spark plug was invented, quickly followed in 1903 by the next major advance, developed by a German engineer, Robert Bosch. This was the high-tension magneto system, designed to produce a controlled spark, which ignited the vapours in the combustion chamber at exactly the right time. The combination of the magneto and the sparking plug was quickly adopted by the major manufacturers. This ignition system, now almost 100 years old, remains the basis of all car and motorbike ignition systems to this day.

At the beginning of the century, motorcycle development was being pioneered in continental Europe, where roads were generally free of speed restrictions and also the European manufacturers eagerly employed designers and engineers.

The ever-present quest for speed increased demands on

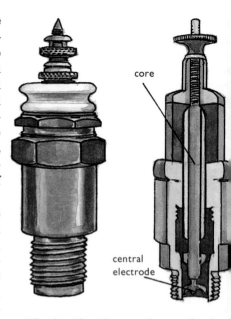

The inside of an early spark plug showing the core and central electrode

8

ike technology, and the intro-
uction of the V-section rubber
nd canvas or leather drive
elts was followed by improved
uspension in the form of the
ront-end parallel-slider fork
hat had compression springs.
Developed by Alfred Drew in
906, these greatly improved
he handling and steering
roperties of the racing bike, in
ddition to providing greater
omfort.

The next major improvement
vas to the gearing. Enter Oscar
Iandstrom and George Hendee,
vho were the founders of the
ndian Motorcycle Company of
Springfield, Massachusetts.

Below: *the Indian Racer of 1908,
beautifully restored*

They had been experimenting
with a two-speed centre shaft
transmission, which incorporated a clutch. They were able
finally to integrate this with a
drive chain and rear-wheel gear
sprockets, to replace the belt
system. These Indian V-twin
four-strokes therefore broke
dramatically onto the motorcycle scene when they took the
first three places in the 1911
Manx Tourist Trophy (TT).

The increased activity in the
marketing of motorcycles
inevitably led to smaller companies specialising in parts
rather than the finished production motorcycle, and this in
turn led to a plethora of very
small companies or individuals
assembling these off-the-shelf
parts into very marketable
machines. Equally inevitably,
these small companies came
and went very quickly, unable
to keep abreast of the design
and engineering improvements
until, with the onset of the
First World War, they disappeared and so the focus of
motorcycle innovation shifted
to the USA. In particular, the
Indian Motorcycle Company,
which had been founded in 1901,
in 1913 introduced rear suspension and in 1914 was able to
boast the largest motorcycle
factory in the world. Harley-
Davidson, by 1914, had dropped

the belt drive and a year later introduced the first three-speed transmission. Other prominent market leaders in the USA were William Henderson's ACE company, which had developed a four-cylinder inline engine, and Excelsior. Other developments to be born in the USA at this time were the twist-grip throttle control, the drum brake on the rear wheel, the foot-operated clutch, and the starter-motor.

COMPETITION

However, pioneering American motorcycle companies did not have it all their own way. They did, after all, have Mr Henry Ford to contend with. In the halcyon days (for the privileged) before the First World War, few people indeed were affluent enough to be able to afford the automobiles then being hand-built, mainly by former carriage makers to the rich. Some of the upwardly mobile young workers often purchased a motorcycle in order to join the personal transportation revolution which was just beginning. At the cost of a

Below: *1924 Indian twin-cylinder Daytona Frame with flexi sidecar*

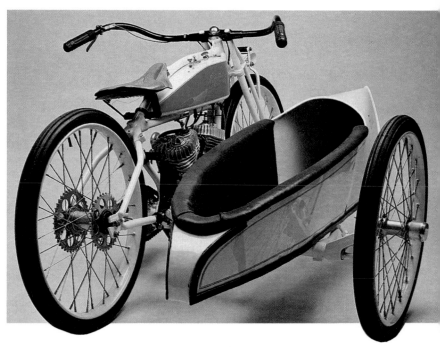

ouple of months' wages, often rranged on easy terms, an arly motorised bicycle could e bought. As often as not, marriage was the spur to upgrade y adding a side-car. Indian, Iarley and many others prospered and did provide basic independent transportation for he masses, but Henry Ford changed all that when he not only introduced mass-produced automobiles at about the time f the First World War, but then progressively lowered the price until it reached the point of

Below: the 1927 BMW R 47 was powered by a 494cc ohv engine

being little more than that of its two-wheeled competitor. Then, as had happened in Europe, motorbike manufacturers across America were bankrupted.

In Europe the demands of war were also to have their impact on motor transport, resulting in the production of harder steels and lighter and stronger alloys, all of which helped to produce a more durable engine with greater power output, capable of improved performance.

Side valves were eventually replaced by pushrod-operated overhead valves, which later were to give way to overhead-

camshaft (ohc) engines. By the mid-1920s both BMW, with its horizontally-opposed twin-cylinder four-strokes, and Moto Guzzi, with its light-weight ohc four-strokes, had made their first trail blazing appearance.

By the late 1920s, Harold Willis had already invented the positive-stop foot-gearchange mechanism, giving a tremend-ous advantage over the slow and laborious hand levers.

Willis was a racing engineer, and it was on the racing circuit where the advantages of his design were most appreciated, as the riders no longer had to dice with each other, steering with one hand while the other wrestled with the gear lever, which was sited beside the petrol tank.

All the components of the modern bike were now being assembled. On the engine front there were the two-stroke engines with rotary valves pioneered by Scott and Vitesse, three-cylinder double ohc four-strokes pioneered by Moto Guzzi, and four-strokes with four valves per cylinder intro-duced by Rudge. Indian had introduced its four-cylinder motor in 1927, and Harley its 290cc (17.7cu in) engine in 1928. The American manufacturers also introduced front brakes,

re-circulating oil systems, th 'buddy' seat and the brake ligl in the early thirties, and by th late thirties, the first suc cessful hydraulically-dampe telescopic front-wheel spring had been fitted by BMW an Norton to their works racers.

THE EFFECTS OF WAR

By the very end of the 1930s, th European motorcycle industr was in a healthy state, but wit the outbreak of the Secon World War all that ended, an many of the prestige names c the era such as Brough, Rudge Sunbeam and New Imperial dis appeared. Some switched thei manufacturing to war compc nents, but never returned t manufacture cycles.

Across the Atlantic, it wa quite different. The stock mar ket's crash of 1929 had seen th utter disappearance of most c the country's cycle manufac turers, and by 1939 the tw remaining companies, bot Indian and Harley-Davidson were each approached by th War Department to build special military bike, whic was to be a 500cc or 30cu in twir While tooling up for its Mode 641, Indian based a small 500c bike on its Junior Scout. Wil liam S Harley had other ideas Telling the War Departmen that its specification wa

*bove: **in full battle dress, a
Harley-Davidson WLA of 1942
intage; rigid frame, chain drive,
V-twin 750cc with three-speed
transmission***

inadequate, he modified the
Forty-five, which was first
introduced in 1928.

Harley was right: the grossly
under-powered Indian-built
00s soon proved to be of very
little practical use, while 88,000
Harley WLAs were produced in
dozens of versions and widely
used by all of the major Allied
forces, with thousands even
being shipped to Russia.

The return of peace saw the
emise of Indian, along with
many of its European brethren,
but others, such as Norton,
Agusta, AJS and NSU picked up
the pieces. Components such as
two-stroke engines and gear-
boxes built by Villiers and
others were sold to small companies, a process reminiscent of
that of 40 years earlier, and the
army of small lightweight
tourers such as Greeves,
Francis-Bennett, DKW, Barnet
Norman, and SM took to the
streets.

One of the most successful
postwar lightweights was the
BSA Bantam, based on a DKW
design. A 123cc single-cylinder
two-stroke three-speed, this
was manufactured in its thou-

13

sands from 1948. It featured petroil lubrication, and flywheel magneto ignition, a solid rear subframe and front telescopic forks, which were undamped.

Unfortunately, the British motorcycle industry grew complacent in the 1950s, and by the early 1960s there were signs that the sales success both at home and abroad enjoyed in the previous decade was beginning a downturn. The industry had failed to invest sufficiently in new engineering and design technology and had also failed to recognise the change in public demand.

The scooter concept 30 years on; a 1993 Vespa T5 manufactured by Piaggio

By 1960, NSU 50cc mopeds ha brought about the demise of th British auto-cycle industr and this was followed by th Italian Vespa and Lambret scooter invasion, which wit their step-through design we acceptable to female ride because they were easy 1 mount and dismount an ridable while wearing a ski and ordinary shoes. The effe in a short three-year peric upon the British motorcyc industry was tremendou Although BSA and Triump embarked hurriedly on scooter programme, they we too late and met with little su cess, while they saw the Italia market leaders gain not ju acceptance but become high fashionable in a predominant middle-class market. Finall all this seemed to be happenir at the very time when tw wheels were under attack agai from four.

This time though, it was n

Vespa T5

Engine: 123.54cc two-stroke single cylinder
Bore and stroke: 55×52mm (2.15×2.03in)
Transmission: four-speed
Ignition: electronic
Performance: top speed 86.89km/h (54mph)

*riel, established in 1898, in
929 produced the 'Squariel'
00cc four with a highly unusual
quare cylinder configuration
nd single overhead camshaft.
'he Square Four, designed by
'dward Turner, had a ball and
oller bearing engine and
orizontally-split crankcase.
oring the engine produced
00cc capacity in 1931; a 1,000cc
quare Four with pushrod power
nit and plain bearings was
unched in 1936, and in 1956,
e luxury roadster above. With
top speed of 169km/h
105mph), it developed 42bhp at
800rpm and was in production
the end of Ariel*

the enterprising Mr Ford, but British designer Alec Issigonis and his 850cc Mini, conspiring to take away yet another large chunk of the British motorcycle market. By now America had only Harley-Davidson left, and Britain was only a little better off. AJS held on until 1969, but its range had been seriously reduced from 1961. The early 1960s also saw the end of Ariel, decreed uneconomic to continue with production by its parent BSA, which itself had become history by 1972. The Yorkshire-based Panther died in 1966, sandwiched between Vincent and Royal Enfield.

THE JAPANESE REVOLUTION

Meanwhile, Japan was happening. The Japanese market was flourishing at home, and demand for two-wheeled transportation was huge. Soichiro Honda had bought a batch of army-surplus two-strokes in 1946 for use converting bicycles to mopeds; by 1949, he had developed his first motorcycle and by 1951 was selling 250 a week.

Part of Honda's success was that he did not rest on his laurels, as had the British. He developed a four-stroke as a stablemate for his two-stroke

Below: *the Honda Dream D Type of 1949 was powered by a 98cc two-stroke*

machine, he developed a step through in 1952, and in 1953 the factory was retooled. I the face of bankruptcy, he vigorously continued to ge production of the 90cc four stroke up to 1,000 per month.

In 1954, Soichiro Honda vis ted the Isle of Man TT race and while he watched Norto take the Senior TT ahead of th Italians and AJS dominate th Junior race, he made up hi mind to promote his machine to a world market by means c the *Grand Prix*. Honda returne to the Isle of Man in 1959 wit his first race team, and cam back the following year, havin learnt much from his 1959 visi five of his six 125cc machine finished the course.

Japanese street bikes wer still quite uncomfortable an

cidedly basic in design, but ey did come with added tras such as wing-mirrors, shing indicators, electric arters and toolkits. Slowly onda, together with Suzuki d Yamaha, began to domi- te the world lightweight otorcycle market, while the ritish kept their blinkers mly on and as one by one they ent out of business. It is easy criticise an expiring manu- cturing industry, but the akers did not lose out to fair competition, they disap- ared like dinosaurs because ey did not develop, invest or en understand the transport olution or conditions in their me market, let alone on the

broader world-wide horizon.

On the big bike front, they simply made slight modifica- tions to existing designs and overbored cylinder diameters to increase capacity, added a twin carburettor or modified the camshaft profiles and con- verted basic street machines into sports models. Outdated designs suffered from these stresses, and the riders from discomfort from the vibration.

Enter Honda yet again, when in 1969 it launched the all-new CB750, with a four-cylinder ohc five-speed which it claimed to have put together from the drawing board to production in six months. Smooth, powerful and very fast, the CB750 was in a different league from the three- cylinder Triumph Trident and BSA Rocket-3.

elow: *Honda's early entry in the med Isle of Man TT Race*

17

ROAD RACING

he first road races were held in urope, with motorcycles able) compete on the open roads etween Paris and the major rench cities such as Bordeaux nd Marseilles.

Meanwhile, in the UK the rst motorcycle races were ctually held on bicycle tracks nat had been established in ondon and Birmingham. In)04, the Royal Automobile lub approached the autho- ties on the Isle of Man to ask ermission to stage trials on he Island. The Isle of Man, like ontinental Europe, placed no peed limits on its roads. These aces were to be sponsored by he American newspaper mag- ate Gordon Bennett. When ermission had been granted, a imilar request was made by he Auto-Cycle Club (A-CC) for he holding of eliminator trials)r the 1905 *Coupe Interna- ionale.*

The trials, though receiving ttle support, were a success nd were won by J S Campbell ding a 6hp Ariel-JAP. The ritish team went on to com- ete, though it was woefully utclassed, in International

aryl Beattie on his Rothmans- Ionda in the 1993 World 'hampionship

Cup races, which were held near Paris. The following year, another British team was entered and the races were held at Putzan in Austria, but the event ended in confusion and disarray, resulting in the disso- lution of both the governing body and the races. On their journey back to England, the members of the team and the Auto-Cycle Club determined to stage races similar to those of the International Cup. The Marquis de Mouzilly St Mars, who had been on the interna- tional jury of the Cup races, agreed to provide a trophy for the winner, but the British government refused to close public roads for the event. For- tunately the Manx government agreed. The A-CC quickly drew up regulations which initially were not too limiting, allowing

Václav Vondrich on a CCR, winner of the 1905 **Coupe Internationale**

for just two classes, twin and single-cylinder, with no limit to engine capacity or machine weight. They did, however, impose fuel limits, of 144km (90 miles) per 4.5461 litres (1 Imp/1.2 US gal) for the singles and 120km (75 miles) for the twins.

A suitable course was selected, with the start at St John's, which consisted of 10 laps with a compulsory 10-minute rest for the riders, in which they were to refuel after the fifth lap, totalling 253km (158 miles). The first race was held on 28 May 1907, contested by 25 riders, who set off in pairs at one-minute intervals. There were ten finishers, and the winner of the single-cylinder class was Charlie Collier riding a JAP-engined Matchless, at an average speed of 61.15km/h (38.22mph). The twin-cylinder event was won by Ron Fowler on a Peugeot powered Norton.

The following year, the A-C ruled that none of the bikes could have the added assistance of pedal power, and the fuel allowance was also cut. The race was won by Jack Marshall at an average speed of 64.78km/h (40.49mph).

Left: *the start of the Isle of Man TT in 1908, and* **below** *winner of the twin-cylinder class, Harry Reed, with his DOT*

The Isle of Man TT Races were becoming popular, and the following year with the capacity of the singles limited to 500cc and of the twins to 750cc, the number of competitors had doubled. Although Charlie Collier won easily on his new V-twin Matchless at 78.4km/h (49mph), it was an Indian V-twin that came in second.

The initial St John's circuit was used for the last year in 1910, with 80 entrants. Lap speeds were now up to 85.04km/h (53.15mph), while manufacturers had begun to realise the advantages of testing their new ideas and machines under arduous race conditions which would lead to further experimentation and developments.

The A-CC introduced the Mountain Course for 1911, a 60.75km (37.75-mile) circuit, which included a long 426m (1,400ft) climb up the eastern side of Snaefell. The event was won by Indian, which took the first three places in the Senior race, making full use of its countershaft two-speed gears with chain drive to the rear wheel. O C Godfrey came home first at an average 76.21km/h (47.63mph).

The post-First World War years saw the appearance of paid works riders, and as the European motorcycle industry expanded and gathered pace, so it began to organise its own *Grand Prix* events. At this stage, events were still being competed by the development models of some sports street machines; it was not until the late 1930s that the prestige of winning races drove the manufacturers to design road-racing machines that departed radically from the roadster.

The Second World War interrupted road racing for eight years, but by 1947 the pre-War machines had been dusted off, oiled and pushed out onto the track to do battle again, albeit on low-octane 'pool' petrol. Norton and Velocette took up where they had left off, taking the Isle of Man TT honours but the turbochargers developed by BMW and Gilera in the late 1930s were banned by the Federation of International Motorsport (FIM).

Competition winning became all again for the successful manufacturer in the very early 1950s. Gilera developed its 500cc four-cylinder racer, MV Agusta its 500-Quattro, and manufacturers lavished vast sums to fulfil their desire for success on the track; so much so, that the cost soon outstripped the revenue obtained from the extra showroom sales. By the mid-1950s, British manufacturers

Above: *riding a BMW, Schorch Meier was the first foreign rider on a non-English machine to win the 'Senior Race', when he won the 1939 Isle of Man Tourist Trophy Race*

Right: *the Velocette Venom of 1956, an ohv sports roadster with a square 86 × 86mm (3.35 × 3.35in) engine which developed 36bhp at 6,200rpm and a top speed of 152.8km/h (95mph)*

Above: six times in a row, between 1967 and 1974, Klaus Enders and Ralf Engelhardt won the Makers' World Championship for 500cc machines with side-car for BMW

were beginning to withdraw their factory support from works teams, with the Italian Gilera and Moto Guzzi companies following suit in 1957, leaving MV Agusta almost alone on the circuit until the arrival of the Japanese at the Isle of Man in 1961 with their lightweight 250cc racer. The little four-cylinder lapped the TT circuit at a full 159.3km/h (99.58mph), only fractionally slower than the 350cc MV and the 500cc Norton which won the Senior event.

Honda was joined by Yamaha and Suzuki and so a three-cornered battle ensued for the coveted lightweight racing

Top left: *Kevin Schwantz on his way to becoming the 500cc Motor Racing Champion in 1993 on his Suzuki RGV 500*

Right: *racing technology transferred to the street; the Suzuki RGV 250 takes its advanced design straight from the RGV Gamma racer*

Yamaha won the 500cc World Road Race Championship in 1990, 1991 and 1992, and in 1993 the World 250cc Championship went to Tetsuya Haruda in his first-ever year of GP racing. Right *is James Whitham, who* **won the British TT/Superbike Championship and the HEAT 750cc Supercup series in 1993 on a Yamaha YZF 750 SP**

Left: *Australian Wayne Gardner on his 500cc Honda during the 1992 World Championship. Gardner was World Champion in 1987, having been runner-up the previous year. Honda's first 500cc World Championship win fell to Freddie Spencer in 1983, which he followed with a unique double in 1985 when he won both the 250 and 500cc events*

Suzuki RGV250

Country of origin: Japan
Engine: 249cc liquid-cooled two-stroke 90° V2
Carburettor: two 34mm (1.33in) Mikuni TM SS
Output: 45.88kW (62hp) at 11,000rpm; maximum torque 40Nm (29.6ft/lb) at 11,000rpm
Bore and stroke: 56 × 50.6mm (2.18 × 1.97in)
Transmission: six-speed constant mesh Takasago RK520MOZ4 or Daido DID520V2 114-link chain-driven
Brakes: front 300mm (11.7in) floating twin discs; rear 210mm (8.19in) disc
Tyres: front 110/70 R 17 54H; rear 150/60 R 17 66H low-profile radials
Dimensions: length 1,980mm (77.9in); width 690mm (27.2in); seat height 766mm (30.2in); weight 139kg (304lb); fuel tank 16 litres (3.52 Imp/4.23 US gal)
Electronics: Multiple Digital Ignition System (MDIS)
Frame: aluminium double cradle; swinging arm includes a subframe
Suspension: inverted telescopic front fork with 41mm (1.6in) stanchion tubes; rear link-type

Overleaf: *Luca Cadalora, No 3, powers his 250cc Honda into the lead during the 1991 world championship season*

crown, as MV Agusta stood as Europe's hope in the 350 and 500cc classes.

As so often happens in both motor car and motorbike racing, the governing bodies were constantly forced to alter the regulations, so that state-of-the-art technology could be allowed to develop but not to dominate, and to avoid a race becoming a procession. This was happening in the early 1960s, with Honda and Suzuki dominating the lightweight classes to such an extent that the FIM tightened up the regulations in 1967. Because of this, these two Japanese manufacturers withdrew their support in 1967, leaving a clear road for the third Japanese manufacturer, Yamaha, which went on to rule the 125, 250 and 350cc

events and to enjoy over-the counter sales of production racing bikes.

Yamaha's dominance and sales success forced Suzuki back onto the track first in the 1970s, with a successful team led by Barry Sheene, and by the end of the decade Honda was back.

Since the start of the 1970s the Isle of Man TT races with their high record of incidents have been eclipsed by the dominance of the *Grand Prix* World Championships and therefore the public's attention has been diverted to such race-tracks as Hockenheim, Spa and Monza.

Fred Merkel, winner of the first World Superbike Championship in 1988, on a Honda

MOTOCROSS

his rugged and exciting sport races its history back to the arly 1920s, when a Harley-avidson ridden by A B Sparks on a race comprised of two gs over a 48km (30-mile) ourse in Surrey, England. The arly enthusiast used his street achine, probably riding to the eeting on it, stripped bare of ll non-racing essentials such s lights and mudguards. The wo-legged affair would be nterrupted both for lunch and or essential repairs, and the inner would be the rider with he best average placing over he two heats. In the event of a ie, it was then down to time. Motocross, or scrambling as it vas originally known in the JK, had little following or nvestment. However, the new evelopment of the telescopic ront fork and also the hy-raulically damped swinging rm rear suspension provided he manufacturers with the ncouragement to get involved hat they had lacked, and to uild motorcycles that could be idden at high speeds over ough ground with a reasonable egree of stability.

In the 1950s, the term *Moto-ros* was coined by the French nd Belgians, who built special ircuits with both rider and spectator in mind, and the influx of spectators was quickly matched by the interest from the manufacturers who began to enter some works-sponsored teams. Bikes of the early 1950s were primarily large 500cc single-cylinder four-strokes, but they gave way eventually to the new generation of 250cc two-strokes from Husqvarna, CZ and Greeves. Highly tuned and with lightweight suspension systems, they took the fight to the larger machines and 350cc two-strokes appeared, able to compete in senior events. Even despite the FIM rulings, the Matchless, the AJS and the Norton four-strokes became history almost over-night.

Another effect of the arrival of the competitive two-stroke was its price, and this allowed thousands of bystanders to take up the sport for them-selves. Motocross as a sport grew rapidly, indeed at a greater pace than any other motorcycle sport right across Europe, and hence was the focus of tremendous interest from the manufacturers.

The enthusiasm crossed to the United States, and there too the market boomed, not unnoticed by the Japanese manufacturers, who had until now concentrated on their road

racing activities where they dominated; they saw motocross as another potential sales area and went for it.

Suzuki was first, buying the services of World Champion Roger DeCoster and Joel Robert, embarking on a crash development programme and although highly expensive it paid off. In its first season, Suzuki won the World 250cc

British multi-champion Dave Thorpe won the 500cc Motocross Works title in 1985 and 1986, and Georges Jobe was World Champion in 1987. Eric Geboers, above, sole winner of world titles in all three solo motocross classes, was 250cc Champion in 1987 and 500cc champ in 1988, the same year Jean-Michel Bayle right, gave Honda its first 125cc world title

Motocross Championship with motorcycle that weighed in at just 72.5kg (160lb). It took the title for the following two years, before moving up to the 500cc class, where it was to meet with equal success.

In the interest of sport, the FIM fought back, imposing a minimum weight restriction of 95kg (210lb) and the advantages gained by having the ultra-light titanium frames was gone. It was now down to the manufacturers to find other ways of gaining an advantage over their competitors, and the 1970s saw renewed efforts to improve the frame even more.

Yamaha developed the tri-angulate rear fork, suspended on a single but very large damping unit, its pivot at the rear of the main frame. The overall effect was to give the Yamaha machine somewhere in the region of 250mm (10in) of suspension movement to both front and rear, with the result that the bikes kept in greater contact with the ground surface. The riders were therefore able to exploit more fully both the power and the flexibility of their engines, which in turn led to greater handling control.

Development continues as ever in this large sector of motorcycle racing, with Yamaha having improved intake and exhaust efficiency for the 1994 YZ125, aimed at improving power delivery throughout the new range in addition to lowering the frame weight by 0.5kg (1lb).

Motocross today can be defined as racing on a closed circuit of 2-3km (1.24-1.86 mile), in which as many as 40 riders start together in a straight line. Events usually last between 10 and 20 minutes. Riders are normally allowed a practice session or two, and on race day will probably participate in up to four events. Children can start on semi-automatic bikes from the age of six, graduating through 80cc machines up t 125cc. Adults enter at 16. Sepa ate classes exist for road-lega trial bikes, off-road/endur bikes, four-wheel quads an sidecars. More and mor interest is now being shown i recently out of date bikes, wit events for twin-shock bike over five years old, and in th *real* pre-65 oldies, usually bille as scramblers.

New machines in race-read condition are offered by mos manufacturers, and costs var from one country to anothe Extras include clothing an race entry fees.

Supercross is motocross on man-made circuit, generall within a sports stadium an usually on a shale surface.

Suzuki has been winning off-road races at the top level for a quarter of a century, with a total of 24 world championship titles. Above is the race-ready Suzuki RM 250 motocross bike

Motocross can be a great deal of fun, and with many manufacturers making race-ready machines the enjoyment is now more available to a greater number of participants

Suzuki RM 250

Country of origin: Japan
Engine: two-stroke water-cooled Automatic Exhaust Timing Control (AETC)
Capacity: 249cc
Output: 39.9kW (53.5hp) at 8,500rpm
Transmission: five-speed
Dimensions: wheelbase 1,465mm (57.68in); seat height 960mm (37.79in); weight 98kg (216.09lb); fuel tank 7.5 litres (1.65 Imp/1.37 US gal)
Suspension: inverted telescopic front link-type; spring preload at rear

The enduro is best described as a long-distance motocross, with time elements and special tests but no mass starts. For the competitor, enduro provides excellent value for money in terms of actual competition riding time, with events taking anything from three to six hours. There are classes for different levels of ability as well as for different grades of machines, and these often vary from one event to another. These bikes are essentially motocross machines, having lights, a wider powerband and chassis modifications, and so prices are comparable.

Beach races, desert races and hare-and-hound events are all variations on the same theme, though these do involve mass starts and a set race time.

Top right: *the KTM Enduro LC4 600 EXC 1993 is the top of the range on offer from KTM-Sportmotorcycle Gesellschaft MBH of Austria and comes in two versions, the EXC illustrated and the EGS street machine*

Bottom right: *Husqvarna, now part of the Italian Cagiva group, offers the TC 610 illustrated and the TE-designated enduro variant, which has a six-speed (instead of five) chain-driven transmission*

KTM Enduro LC4 600 EXC 1993

Country of origin: Austria
Engine: liquid-cooled four-stroke single with four valves
Capacity: 553cc
Carburettor: 38mm (1.48in) Dell'Orto PHM
Bore and stroke: 95 × 78mm (3.7 × 3.04in)
Transmission: five-speed O-ring chain-driven
Brakes: front 260mm (10.14in) disc with double piston and organic pads; rear 220mm (8.58in) disc with single piston and organic pads
Tyres: front 90/90 21 Metzeler Unicross; rear 140/80 18 MCE (130/90 18 Unicross)
Dimensions: length 2,340mm (91.26in); width 840mm (32.76in); wheelbase 1,500mm plus or minus 10mm (58.5in plus or minus 0.39in); clearance 360mm (14.04in); seat height 960mm (37.44in); weight 123kg (271lb); fuel tank 10.5 litres (2.31 Imp/2.77 US gal)
Frame: chrome-molybdenum-steel main frame and sub-frame
Suspension: White Power USD multi-adjuster front fork with 290mm (11.31in) wheel travel; White Power integral shock absorber with reservoir and 290mm (11.31in) travel at rear

TRIALS

Aprilia Climber 280 R 1993

Trials riding has for long been regarded as one of motorcycle racing's safest, if not slowest, sports events. Today's purpose-built bikes have a clearance underneath the bottom of the frame of at least 250mm (10in), and although engines vary in size from 125 to 400cc, they were designed to produce maximum torque at the lower end of the rev scale. Equipped with a wide-ratio gearbox of up to six speeds, the bikes must conform to street usage specifications and in the UK must be registered and taxed.

Unlike the *Grand Prix*, the very essence of the trials is balance and control, as opposed to outright speed.

Courses vary tremendously, but generally extend to a distance of 40.225km (25 miles) or more and are split into sections, each of these having three or more sub-sections. These are presided over by marshals who are placed to observe each competitor as he passes through the marked course. The terrain of the course should include steep slippery muddy banks, uneven rocks and boulders to be traversed, trees and prominent roots to be negotiated, and rushing streams crossed over. To say the least,

Country of origin: Italy
Engine: two-stroke liquid-cooled single-cylinder
Capacity: 276.6cc
Carburettor: 26mm (1.014in) Dell'Orto PHBH CS oval section
Bore and stroke: 76×61mm (2.96×2.38in)
Transmission: six speed, Regina chain-driven
Brakes: front Grimeca floating 183mm (7.14in) disc; rear Grimeca 160mm (6.24in) disc
Tyres: front 2.75×21in Pirelli MT 73; rear 4×18in Pirelli MT 73
Dimensions: length 2,007mm (78.27in); width 845mm (32.96in); clearance 320mm (12.48in); seat height 720mm (28.08in); weight 83kg (183.02lb); fuel tank 3.7 litres (0.814 Imp/0.98 US gal)
Electronics: ignition
Frame: split single beam in chromium steel with light alloy seat support and engine protection plate
Suspension: inverted telehydraulic front fork; Aprilia Progressive System (APS) swinging arm at rear

Right, above: *The 280 R appeared in 1991, taking Tommi Ahvala to the 1992 Trial World Championship*

*Above: **a competitor attempts a typical trials obstacle***

the courses are testing, difficult even hazardous and they must be completed without a foot touching the ground or the bike coming to a stop. Penalty points are accumulated on the following basis: 1 point for putting a steadying foot to the ground, 3 points for using feet while still seated to assist through a section, and 5 points if the motorcycle stops, goes off course or fails to complete any of the sections.

Trials riding existed as an amateur sport up to the 1960s, a hobby that came into being after the First World War, when despatch riders had learnt their skills on the muddy, rutted, scarred fields of Europe. Early machines were no more than roadster motorcycles fitted with knobbly tyres to provide additional grip.

The very first purpose-built machines had been built by Greeves, which produced in collaboration with DOT in the late 1950s a new lightweight two-stroke motorcycle using a Villiers engine, but the real breakthrough in trials bikes came in 1961, when the successful trials rider Sammy Miller left BSA to design a trials bike for Bultaco, a small Spanish motorcycle manufacturer. Using Bultaco's 250cc single-cylinder two-stroke, he built the Bultaco Sherpa, which was to become the benchmark for all future trials bikes. The success of the bike brought about the trials revolution across both Europe and America.

The FIM, international controlling body for motorcycle sport, granted championship status in 1966 to a series of events in Europe, the first of which was won by Don Smith in 1967 on his works Greeves, but Sammy Miller took the crown from him for Bultaco the following year. Smith joined another Spanish company, Montesa, and with the two-

Betamotor Zero

Country of origin: Italy
Engine: two-stroke liquid-cooled single cylinder with reed valve fuel supply
Capacity: 260.7cc
Carburettor: 26mm (1.01in) Mikuni VM 26/208
Bore and stroke: 76 × 57.5mm (2.96 × 2.24in)
Transmission: six-speed chain-driven
Brakes: front and rear discs
Tyres: front 2.75 × 21in; rear 4 × 18in tubeless
Dimensions: length 2,030mm (79.17in); width 830mm (32.37in); wheelbase 1,325mm (51.68in); clearance 350mm (13.65in); seat height 710mm (27.69in); fuel tank 3.8 litres (0.84 Imp/1 US gal)
Electronics: ignition
Frame: aluminium deltabox
Suspension: 36mm (1.4in) front fork with adjustable compression and extension, rear adjustable shock absorber

The Betamotor Zero 1993 model is illustrated above right. The USA is Betamotor's best customer, but in Japan the company is best known for trial machines. Unlike most Italian competitors, since the 1960s its engines have been manufactured in house, along with other basic components

stroke he designed and built for the company took the title back the following year, only to lose it to Miller again in 1970.

In 1975, the FIM finally announced that the European event would be given World Championship status and big money at last found its way into the sport.

Trials bikes are generally priced slightly below moto-cross machines, and in addition clothing and entry fees do tend to be less. Classes exist for riders of differing ability and for types of machine – modern, twin-shock, pre-65, sidecars and trail bikes.

The popular Betamotor at work in the trials competition field

TIME TRIALS

Known as enduros in the United States, these six-day events are run as time trials and are probably motorcycling's toughest sport on both the man and the machine. Competitors set off at one-minute intervals, and must pace themselves against the clock to average a set speed. The checkpoints are located throughout the course and each one must be reached on time, with points lost for late arrival. Distances and terrain vary, but 300km (186 miles) per day is not an uncommon target to be set, much of it over rugged countryside.

The one major snag to this though, is that no outside assistance many be given to the riders, and thus any running repairs have to be made at the roadside. Each competitor must carry his own equipment and so to be fully equipped means carrying a spare chain, brake lever, clutch lever, inner tube and compressed air bottle, and a full array of tools just in case. Needless to say, the rider must also be an able mechanic if he is to stand any chance of winning.

One of the oldest-established time trials is the International Six Days Trial (ISDT), first held in 1913 with the intention of showing the world just what a reliable form of transport the

Above: 1977 246cc ČZ (TS twin). After 1945, ČZ became part of the nationalised Czechoslovakian motorcycle industry and also became commercially connected with Jawa

Left: 123cc MZ (TS Model 125/G) of 1966, as used by the national DDR team for six-day trials

motorcycle was. Since then, the courses have become more arduous, but even post-First World War the emphasis was on reliability. From 1924 the ISDT was held in a different country each year, with the award of the Silver Vase Trophy to national teams of three riders who were to be entered on foreign-made machines. Since the Second World War, bike specifications for these trials have improved tremendously with the Czechoslovakian JAWA/CZ and the East German MZ two-strokes dominating the European scene throughout the 1960s and 1970s, with their factory teams almost invincible. Current six-day trial regulations only allow ten minutes of maintenance work on the bikes per day, in addition to any time won by having arrived early at the checkpoints. All of the bikes are locked up overnight and closely guarded to discourage any temptation to tinker.

41

SPEEDWAY

A speedway meeting is normally comprised of 13 four-lap races, with two teams, each of seven riders, who interchange order so that two riders at a time compete against a different pair from the opposing team in every race. The scoring works on 3 points for a win, two for second place and one for third, with the team with most points winning the match. Teams are organised into leagues or divisions, and during the season the riders compete two or three times a week at home or away on specially-prepared oval tracks of shale.

Speedway has its roots in the United States, being run originally on pony-trotting tracks. The bikes they used were big 1,000cc Harleys and Indian twins, ridden at full tilt round the ovals to very large crowds. Exciting it may have been, but it was also dangerous, and it wasn't long before restrictions limited capacity to 500cc. As ever, innovation began to replace raw power, and the more daring riders began sliding their machines broadside into the corners, while leaving the throttle still fully open.

The sport had spread to Australia by the mid-1920s, and in 1926 a 400m (1,312.4ft) track was operational in Brisbane, where one Cecil Brown is said to have developed the now mandatory leg-trailing broadside riding style.

In 1927, the first dirt track meeting was held in England at the Camberley Club in Surrey. Unfortunately it did not meet with its hoped-for success, the organisers having used not only a dull sand surface but run the event clockwise round the circuit, completely opposite to all ideas current, then and now. They did get it right however a month later in Manchester, and it wasn't long before the sport had been accepted and manufacturers were again starting to innovate so as to meet the new demands of a new sport.

One of the first successful bikes was the 500cc single-cylinder JAP four-stroke. It had a short wheelbase and a solid rear-end frame, minimum movement sprung front forks and no gearbox was required. Such was its suitability that the JAP-engined machines ruled the circuits for almost 30 years, being finally eclipsed by the ESO (later JAWA) 500cc four-strokes from Czechoslovakia during the 1960s, which themselves were able to rule the roost on the world speedway circuits for almost a decade.

After the Second World War it was Sweden, in the shape of Ove Fundin, who captured the solo World Speedway Championship title on five occasions, and New Zealanders Ivan Mauger and Barry Briggs, each with four World Championships, that gave speedway its really international flavour.

It was the British Westlake Engineering Company which upset the scene in 1974 with its new 500cc four-valve single-cylinder; not only beating JAWA on the track, they also offered the engine over the counter, whereas JAWA's were reserved purely for the selected few.

Both grass-track and ice racing are similar to speedway, and both use machines of a similar design. Grass-track racing is undoubtedly a forerunner of the speedway, but was never organised along proper professional lines, and nor did it ever reach the popularity of speedway, that once boasted being Britain's top spectator sport. However, grass-track has proved itself most useful as a breeding ground for the more spectacular shale ovals, which being held indoors, are not at the mercy of the weather.

Ice racing is altogether another dimension, developed in the sub-zero temperatures of

Simon Wigg, triple world Long Track Champion

Eastern Europe on frozen lakes, where riders equip themselves with thick knee pads. Originally old car tyres were used, and as the bikes bank at incredible angles round the corners, the riders' knees skate along the ice. The bikes used are similar to the basic speedway machine, 500cc four-strokes with no brakes, a clutch that is used purely for starting, a throttle to control the speed and, most important of all, the major difference to their sister bikes is the multitude of 40mm (1.5in) needle-sharp steel spikes which are fitted to the tyres and which bite into the surface of the ice circuit, allowing the riders to corner at such incredible angles to the ice.

DRAG RACING

To describe a drag bike is not easy; it can be anything, and the only thing they do have in common is a long low chassis, devoid of rear suspension, and a wide, flat rear tyre. The rest is open to the technical beliefs of the rider. To describe the event is easier; all you have to do is to go in a straight line for 400m (0.25 mile) in the shortest time possible.

Drag racing has, however, probably been responsible for more innovation and technical wizardry than any other race form. At a single open meeting you may find bikes with one, two, or three engines, supercharged or unsupercharged, single speed or multi-speed transmissions, but one thing is sure: these are beloved works of art, on which many hours have been spent in preparation for a mere few seconds' worth of an exhilarating rocket-like blast of power.

Just as the quarter-mile race had been the measure of American muscle cars, so it was in the early days of drag racing for the bikers who used standard road-going machines against the clock. Gradually frames were lightened in an effort to obtain that extra ounce of acceleration.

Already the art of mixing and matching had begun, as heavy duty front forks were replaced on 500cc models with those from 50cc models, very small drum brakes were used on the front, smaller fuel tanks were fitted and bit by bit today's dragster took shape as the competition became more fierce. Super charging helped, the use of methanol fuel helped, and wide flat-sectioned 'slick' tyres which were covered in soft tacky high-hysteresis rubber and developed by the Avon Tyre company, helped grip the road

Frames became stretched and lower and bikes got faster and faster and the time for the quarter-mile dropped further until with the introduction of his single speed machine

without any gearbox at all, Alf Hagon rode his 1,300cc JAP V-twin from start to tape in less than 10 seconds. This had dropped to 7.8 seconds by the end of the 1970s, as riders tried every device imaginable to shave that smallest fraction of a second off the record. Burnouts became commonplace; this is when the rear wheel is spun to heat up the tyre until it is hot and sticky and therefore at its most adhesive. Petrol is then set alight around the tyre before the clutch is dropped and the bike freed.

Inevitably drag racing had become expensive and sponsorship was essential unless you just wanted to turn up at the meeting on your roadster, take off what bits you could, fit the rubbers and go for it.

Basically if you're going to be a biker then at least today there is ample opportunity for you to go out and enjoy it whatever your taste.

Werner Brückle driving his 1,400cc Kawasaki *illustrated above* took 1993's Le Mans 200m (218.73yd) drag title, covering the distance in 5.21 seconds, which translates to a top speed of 216.2km/h (134mph) or zero to 200km/h (124mph) in 5 seconds. The Kawasaki delivers 281kW (380hp) with nitrous oxide injection, which allows this kind of acceleration orgy via an 11-inch rear tyre and a very sensitive clutch. Brückle claims to use only 12 litres (2.69 Imp/3.17 US gal) of fuel in an entire racing season.

APRILIA
Noale, Italy

One of the newer Italian bike manufacturers; Aprilia, unlike Bimota, has concentrated on the manufacture of scooters and smaller bikes of 125cc capacity. Major landmarks in the company history are as follows:

1968 Ivano Beggio joined the bicycle company founded by his father Alberto, and decided to start the production of small off-road mopeds, along with the range of bicycles already manufactured. The interest in competition intensified with this expansion, that changed Aprilia to a racing-oriented company.

1975 the first motorcycles were built. These were later to become the company's most important source of profit.

1980 the first steps were taken in the transformation of Aprilia into a company devoted to research, development and design. Components were all made abroad, while the final assembly of the motorcycle was carried out in the factory.

1990 Aprilia had become well

Below: *the successful Aprilia Scarabeo scooter is powered by a 49.3cc two-stroke*

Right: *the 1994 Pegaso 650 model is the largest in Aprilia's range*

Aprilia Pegaso 650

Country of origin: Italy
Engine: four-stroke liquid-cooled single-cylinder with five radial valves
Capacity: 651.8cc
Carburettor: two 33mm (1.29in) Mikuni BSTs with vacuum
Output: 37kW (50hp) at 7,000rpm; maximum torque 53Nm (39ft/lb) at 6,500 rpm
Bore and stroke: 100 × 83mm (3.9 × 3.24in)
Transmission: five speed chain-driven
Brakes: front 300mm (11.7in) disc; rear 220mm (8.58in) disc
Tyres: front 100/90 × 19; rear 140/70 × 17
Dimensions: length 2,197mm (85.68in); width 830mm (32.37in); wheelbase 1,467mm (57.21in); clearance 311mm (12.13in) minimum; seat height 890mm (34.71in); weight 157kg (346.19lb); fuel tank 14 litres (3.08 Imp/3.69 US gal)
Performance: top speed over 175 km/h (108.68 mph)
Electronics: ignition
Frame: aluminium double beam, front part steel boxed section acts as oil tank
Suspension: 41mm (1.6in) inverted front fork; swinging arm with single shock absorber at rear; 210mm (8.19in) travel front and rear

47

established at home, and has become further committed to the world market, with the stated aim of having more than 50% of sales turnover from the export trade, by early 1995. Alongside the motorcycle production, Aprilia had diversified into manufacturing scooters with great success, and also marketed this product all over Europe. The company was represented in the Road Racing World Championship in the 125cc and 250cc classes, as well as in the Trial and Enduro World Championships.

1992 Aprilia gained the title of World Champion in the 125cc Road Racing and Trial classes.

1994 development of new urban vehicles, mainly scooters, is expected to continue, and at the end of the year the new 250cc hypersport road bike will be introduced. The sports activities will also be increased by venturing into the bigger bikes category for the 500cc Road Racing World Championship.

The RS 125 SP 94 is the latest sports production bike to be offered by Aprilia, and draws on the experience gathered on the track during the 1993 championship season, during which Aprilia won two Italian titles

BIMOTA
Rimini, Italy

Bimota is located in the very heart of both four and two-wheel motormania. Its neighbours include Ferrari, Lamborghini, Maserati, Iso Rivolta and Bugatti on the four-wheel front, and Pininfarina on the design side, while their two-wheel competitors include Ducati, Moto Morini, Malanca, Malagati and Minaralli. The passion does not stop there either; the area also boasts the Formula 1 motor racing teams of Ferrari, Minardi and Lamborghini while also being the home of such famous motorcycle racers as Renzo Pasolini, Louis Reggiani, Mario Lega, Proni, Walter Villa, P F Chili, Otello Buscherini, Luca Cadalora, Louis Capirossi and Bruno Casanova. To service this amazing array of motor exponents are the racing tracks of Imola and Misano.

It is hardly surprising then that the three people who had formed Bimota, Valerio Bianchi, Giuseppe Morri and Massimo Tamburini, giving the company the first two letters of each of their names, although originally involved since 1966 in the heating and air-conditioning industry, should take their first steps in 1972 towards involvement in motorcycles.

Morri and Tamburini wer active motorcyclists, Tam burini himself being an eage rider. He was involved in a se ious crash on the Misam track. By this time Bianchi ha left the company but from th remains of Tamburini's Hond 750 four, Bimota built its firs motorcycle, which was com pleted on the Thursday evenin in time for qualifying practic for the Imola 200. Luigi Anell was invited to ride, but he wa unable to achieve a good resul and opted to partner Robert Gallina, riding a Honda 75 four. Despite working fran tically through the followin nights in order to make th adjustments that Anelli ha suggested, the bike was stil not acceptable.

The following year Bimot designed and manufactured th Paton 500, which was tuned b Peppino Pattoni and raced b Anelli and Gallina.

In 1974, a new Bimota bik made its *début* at Módena rac track, but despite excellen practice results, never finishe the race. As the season pr gressed, however, things bega to improve. Giuseppe Elemen joined the team, and achieved third place behind Giacom Agostini and Walter Villa, wit Gallini in fourth place. Tw

ictories followed for Silvio
Grassetti, Zeltweg and Imola.

Owing to a terrible accident
o Elementi in 1975, the official
Bimota team was withdrawn
rom racing, but not before new
tar Johnny Cecotta and Proni
nd Lega had gained victories.
During 1975 the company was
ble to vacate its 100m² (119.6sq
d) factory to move into larger
lant of some 1,500m² (1,794sq
d). The next year it was back
ontesting the 500cc class with
Vanes Francini and the 350cc
lass with Paolo Scattolari, but
nsuccessfully.

However Barsi won the Ital-
an championship with the
Bimota-designed 250cc Harley-
Davidson that, ridden by
Valter Villa, went on to win
hree World Championships.
Bimota also produced its first
treet machine in 1977, the SB 2
50cc, which was made in co-
peration with SAIAD, the
talian importers of Suzuki.
Meanwhile, on the race track,
Bimota won both the 250cc and
he 500cc Italian Champion-
hips, and the YB 2 250/350cc
acing bike was introduced.

The popular KB1 went into
roduction in 1978, and Bimota
vent on to produce no fewer
han 1,000 units. The YB 3 made
ts début at Misano, ridden by a
oung Randy Mamola, and in
May Marco Lucchinelli and

Rougerie took the YB 3 to the
top by winning the GP world
championship. The following
year saw the return of the official Bimota team to the *Grand
Prix* circuit with the help of
Adriatica. The riders were
Randy Mamola, Eric Saul and
Massimiani, while Fernandez
and Rougerie rode privately-
entered Bimotas.

The same year the SB 3
1,000cc was launched, but it was
in 1980 that Bimota really
arrived, with the winning of the
350cc Riders World Championship and the Manufacturers
World Championship to add to
the two Italian Championships.

The new plant at via Monte-
scudo went into production in
1980, when the company went
public. The HB 2 900cc was
launched at the end of the following year, but Bimota first
scaled down and then withdrew
from racing, following a serious
crash in the *Grand Prix* in
which team leader John
Ekerold was killed.

Massimo Tamburini left the
company in 1983, and there was
a concomitant major scaling
down of its racing activity.

**Overleaf: *the new and
revolutionary Bimota Tesi 1D
chassis, that radically changes
the front suspension and steering
system***

Bimota TESI 1D

Above: *the fully-clothed Tesi 1I*

Engine: four-stroke centrifugal liquid-cooled 90° V2 desmo
Capacity: 904cc
Carburettor: integrated ignition and injection system
Output: 86.6kW (117bhp) at 9,000rpm; maximum torque 105Nm (77.7ft/lb) at 7,500rpm
Bore and stroke: 92 × 68mm (3.59 × 2.65in)
Transmission: six-speed with dry multiple-disc clutch
Brakes: front twin fully-floating 320mm (12.48in) discs, rear single 230mm (8.97in) disc, with hydraulic control
Tyres: front 120/70 ZR 17 Michelin TX 11 TL; rear 180/55 ZR 17 Michelin TX 11 TL
Performance: top speed 255km/h (158mph)

Bimota concentrated more the design of the first prototy TESI machine, using the Hon V4 400cc engine. Continui financial constraints throus 1984 eventually resulted in complete restructuring of t company in 1985, with the full developed TESI all ready f production and the launch the first completely Itali Bimota, the DB1.

Emerging from receiversh in 1986, the company was able enter into a sales and purcha agreement with Yamaha, wi the latter to supply Bimo with engines. These enabled to win the TT FI World Cha pionship in 1987 with Virgin Ferrari, plus two Italian Cha onships and victory in the 000km (621 miles) Monza. By ne end of the year, both the B 4 and the YB 6 had been ntroduced.

By 1988, the company still had nly 38 employees, yet the YB 4 on the Italian Championship nd the following year, with the ppointment of Pierluigi Maroni as technical director. The ESI made its *début* at Misano, oming second to world chamion Meskil and his Honda C30.

The TESI was officially aunched in 1990, powered by a ucati engine, and on the track he company took four Italian hampionships in the 600cc and 50cc classes. The YB and the El urano were exhibited at the 991 Milano show, the latter the astest motorcycle in the world vith 164ps and a top speed of 85km/h (177mph). Back at the orkbench, testing was underay on the new 500cc V-twin, ith direct fuel injection.

Bimota has now amassed ome 350 victories on the race rack, including 22 Italian hampionships, a remarkable chievement for a young comany which has survived hrough such radical changes nd precarious financial straits gainst competition from uch more strongly placed and stablished competitors.

Bimota Furano

Country of origin: Italy
Engine: four-stroke liquid-cooled four-cylinder inline DOHC with five valves per cylinder
Capacity: 1,002cc
Carburettor: integrated ignition and injection system
Output: 121kW (164bhp) at 10,500rpm; maximum torque 120Nm (88.8ft/lb) at 9,250rpm
Bore and stroke: 75.7 × 56mm (2.95 × 2.18in)
Transmission: five-speed with oil-bath multiple-disc clutch
Brakes: front twin 320mm (12.48in) floating discs; rear single 230mm (8.97in) disc
Tyres: front 120/70 ZR 17 Michelin TX 11 TL; rear 180/55 ZR 17 Michelin TX 23 TL
Dimensions: length 2,080mm (81.12in); width 750mm (29.25in); wheelbase 1,420mm (55.38in); clearance 120mm (4.68in); seat height 785mm (30.62in); weight 180kg (396.9lb); fuel tank 20 litres (4.4 Imp/5.3 US gal)
Performance: top speed over 280km/h (174mph)
Frame: aluminium alloy

Overleaf: *the fuel-injected Bimota Furano employs many carbon-fibre parts, which helps to reduce overall weight to 180kg (396.9lb)*

55

BMW

BMW's first motorcycle, the R 32, made its world *début* in October 1923 at the Paris Motor show. It was the first vehicle ever developed in the history of Bayerische Motoren Werke, the company which had started in 1916 with the production of aero engines: the history of BMW cars did not begin until 1928.

On 2 January 1917, 33-year-old graduate engineer Max Friz started working for BMW, hired by Josef Popp, then the Director General of BMW.

When he was still employed by Daimler, Max Friz had developed the four-valve racing engine which helped Mercede to win the French Grand Prix i 1914. At BMW he was given th job of designing an entirely ne motorcycle.

Friz had a drawing board an a stove installed in the gues room of his house in Riesenfeld strasse 34, just to the east of th factory. After little more tha four weeks of hard work, i December 1922, he had alread completed his full-scale desigr

The simple but ingeniou idea applied by Friz was to tur round the existing 500cc two cylinder boxer engine. Now th engine was fitted into th motorcycle crosswise rathe than lengthwise, deliberatel

:posing the two cylinders to
ιe wind rushing by in order to
ve efficient cooling.

Max Friz thus developed a
ɔncept already applied by the
ɾitish ABC company, back in
·19, but now went yet a step
ɪrther. He also fitted in the
·ankshaft lengthwise, thus
·oviding direct drive to the
·ansmission, which was posi-
vely connected to the engine.

elow left: *the first BMW
ɪotorcycle, the R 32*

elow right: *between 1923 and
926, a total of 3,100 R 32s were
ɾoduced at the BMW works in
ɪünchen*

Unlike ABC, he did not use a
bevel gear on the transmission
for the chain drive leading to
the rear wheel, but instead continued the drive train in a
straight line, using the drive
shaft leading directly to the
wheel at the rear. Previously
only the Belgian FN company
had employed this kind of drive
system on its motorcycles. The
frame was made of two tubular
sections, the tank being fast-
ened to the two upper frame
tubes.

The first R 32 motorcycles
were delivered to customers
before the end of 1923. Both
power and performance proved
to be quite adequate, the R 32

offering very ample torque and reaching a top speed of well over 90km/h (56mph) thanks to its low weight of 120kg (265lb) and to the low centre of gravity of the boxer engine, as well as the good roadholding provided. The rider had therefore no problems in handling this kind of speed. Production of the R 32 up to 1926 amounted to more than 3,000 units.

Rudolf Schleicher, who joined BMW in October, 1923, designed a light-alloy cylinder head with overhead valves fully encapsulated and thus well protected from dust; it was also well lubricated. These developments were embodied in the 1925 R 37, which developed a output of 16bhp and provide the starting point for BMW racing machines.

BMW set out to break th absolute world speed record fc motorcycles in 1929, using th same R 37 machine in principl but with its new sports engin This had developed 16bhp out c 500cc, and now featured ove head valves in encapsulate aluminium cylinder heads, a well as steel cylinders. In 192 this engine had already bee further developed into th

Below: *a 1927-built R 47 powere by BMW's 494cc ohv engine*

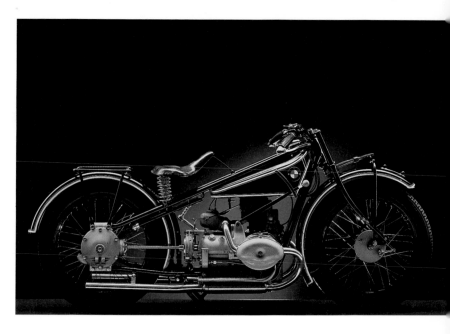

R 47. This had grey cast-iron cylinders and a twin-slide carburettor giving an output of 8bhp. To break the world speed record, the 750cc model was fitted with a compressor for the extra power so essential on the big day of the attempt, 19 September 1929. Riding this special machine on Ingolstädter Landstrasse north of München, Ernst Henne attained an unprecedented top speed of 216km/h (134mph), 10km/h (6.21 mph) more than the previous world record. Almost exactly one year later, on 30 September 1930, Henne again entered the record books, breaking the world speed record for the flying kilometre established by the English rider, Wright, by achieving a top speed of 221 km/h (137mph).

Taking turns, as it were, with British riders, Henne then succeeded time and time again in setting new world records. The final breakthrough came in 1932

Above right: *Rudolf Schleicher (left) congratulates Ernst Henne, who set several world speed records, including one on 28 November 1937 on a 500cc compressor BMW with fairing.*
Right: *He reached 279.5km/h (173.57mph), a record for a 66kW (90hp) flat twin, that stood until 1951*

with a new multiple-disc compressor Rudolf Schleicher had built to provide even more power. Once again, Henne was able to beat the competition; this time it was on a country road in Hungary. Five years later, when riding the latest 80kW (108hp) 500cc compressor machine on the Frankfurt-Darmstadt autobahn, Henne reached his fastest speed ever: a new world record of 279.5km/h (173.3mph) made on 28 November 1937, and remaining in force for no less than 14 years.

By 1935, BMW had already replaced the conventional leaf-spring fork with the first hydraulically dampened front-wheel telescopic fork on the R 12 and R 17, thus introducing a concept which has remained in use to this very day on all motorcycles. The R 5, one of the top-performing machines of its time, was also launched in 1936, with a tubular frame and telescopic fork. Its 500cc power unit developed 24bhp.

In 1938, BMW works rider Georg 'Schorch' Meier won the European Championship. One year later, he was to achieve an even greater sensation, when becoming the first foreigner riding a foreign machine (a BMW) to win the legendary Senior Tourist Trophy on the Isle of Man.

During the Second World War, BMW concentrated on production of the off-road R 75 sidecar machine, with separate sidecar drive and limited-slip differential, eight forward and two reverse gears. The R 75 was initially built at BMW's first factory in München, and then at the Eisenach factory which was lost at the end of the War to the Soviet occupying forces.

BMW's first postwar machine was built in München from parts supplied by dealers. With all the motorcycle production facilities having been moved to Eisenach in the early 1940s on account of the war, the production equipment was out of reach for the München factory.

Accordingly, the managers in there had no choice but to start again from scratch. Machine tools had to be borrowed from other companies to get the production lines working in those enormously difficult times. Another prerequisite was the permit provided by the Allies to build new motorcycles, which were restricted initially to the production of a single-cylinder motorcycle displacing not more than 250cc. The designs required for this purpose, based on the parts collected from dealers all over the country, were available in the summer of 1947, but it was not until shor-

The 1951 R 51/3 featured BMW's new 500cc engine with the suspension and running gear already introduced in 1938

tly before Christmas 1948 that the first R 24 was delivered to its proud owner. A year later, production of this 12bhp machine amounted to almost 10,000 units, followed by 17,000 units in 1950.

This was also the year in which BMW once again was to launch a two-cylinder motorcycle; first the 500cc R 51/2 and then, shortly afterwards, the 590cc R 67.

A new model generation followed in 1955, new standards being set by the all-swinging arm suspension of the R 26, R 50 and R 69. BMW built the RS model in limited numbers for motor sport, with a top speed of 200km/h (125mph). This was also the year in which BMW started to win World Championship titles for motorcycles with sidecars, various teams bringing home this victory for BMW for no less than 20 years non-stop.

Motorcycle registrations in the Federal Republic of Germany amounted to 175,620 units in 1950, with a large proportion of the population using their motorcycles to ride to work. Production of BMW's motorcycles increased continuously over the years, reaching an all-time record figure of 30,000 machines in 1954.

Ten years later, motorcycle retail sales were down to less than 10,000 units a year, no less than 27 manufacturers in West Germany having disappeared from the market. Production of motorcycles by BMW in 1960 totalled approximately 9,500 machines, almost equal to the total number of new motorcycles registered in the Federal Republic of Germany that year.

In the 1960s, most BMW motorcycles went either to the USA or to the police, and in 1969 production was moved from München to Berlin.

Things started to look brighter again in the 1970s. To mark the comeback of the motorcycle, BMW was able to introduce the all-new /5 model series with three engines, displacing 500, 600 and 750cc. In 1973, celebrating 50 years of BMW motorcycle production, the 500,000th machine bearing the white and blue symbol saw the light of day.

By 1973, BMW had gone beyond the 750cc engine size limit previously unbreached for a full 45 years. The R 90/6 and its 67bhp sports counterpart the R 90 S, both featured a 900cc power unit and in 1977 BMW

Left: *the R 90 S, built in 1975. The first BMW machine to displace more than 750cc had appeared on the scene in 1973. With its characteristic cockpit fairing and 67bhp sports engine, the R 90 S was acknowledged as the first superbike*

Above: *the 1976 R 100 RS was a sports tourer that excelled, not only through its engine, which was increased in size from 898cc to 980cc, but also through its full fairing, featured by a production motorcycle for the first time*

launched the first of its 1,000cc machines, the R 100/7, R 100 S and R 100 RS, the latter being the world's first production motorcycle with full fairing. In 1978 the R 100 RS was joined by the R 100 RT tourer, once again optimised in the wind tunnel for perfect streamlining. By this time the motorcycle had definitely returned to the road as a hobby machine, for sports riding, and for motorcycle tours.

In early 1976, BMW AG established a special subsidiary for

all its motorcycle activities; BMW Motorrad GmbH. It was with this new company, led by new executives, that BMW returned to motorcycle racing; this time, however, on the off-road racing scene. The first step was to enter the German Off-Road Championship, for which BMW won the title in both 1979 and 1980. This was also the year in which BMW won the European Championship in the 750cc-plus category, summer 1980 being the time when this successful off-road machine was launched in the market as a refined production enduro designated the R 80 G/S. A special feature of this new machine

which received special atten tion right from the start wa the new single swinging arm the BMW Monolever, with the rear wheel running on a single arm fitted at the side.

When the R 80 G/S entered the Paris-Dakar Rally on 1 Janu

Below: *the R 80 GS, built in 1980 was the first enduro to enter the world market*

Right: *in 1983, Hubert Auriol left won the Paris-Dakar Rally on a BMW for the second time. His team-mate, Belgian rider Gaston Rahier* (right) *won this endurance race on a BMW in 1984 and 1985*

ary 1981, a common joke among participants was that BMW was now trying to get rid of the boxer once and for all in its 58-year history by sending it into the desert; but it was precisely there, in the Sahara, that the boxer benefitted tremendously from its basic concept, developed back in 1923 by Max Friz; a good power-to-weight ratio, absolutely reliable cooling, a very good balance of all masses and moving forces, a low centre of gravity, high continuous output at relatively low engine speeds, superior reliability, endurance, and very simple control and maintenance.

The Frenchman Huber Auriol clinched victory for BMW in the motorcycle category of this toughest rally in the world, open also to cars and even trucks, riding only a slightly more powerful machine (57 instead of 50bhp) than the standard model, with a larger tank (50 litres/11 Imp gal/13.21 US gal) instead of 20 litres/4.4 Imp gal/5.3 US gal). BMW riders Fenouil and Neimer were almost as successful, finishing fourth and seventh and thus enabling BMW to bring home not only an overall win in the motorcycle category but also the team prize.

In the years which followed, BMW motorcycles repeated this proof of their performance three more times, clearly showing the world that no other design principle was able to provide 165km/h (102.5mph) from a powerful 76bhp 1,000cc machine still light enough (175kg/386lb) to win such a gruelling race through the desert. Following Auriol's success in 1981 and 1983, it was a former Motocross World Champion from Belgium, Gaston Rahier, who won this coveted trophy for BMW in 1984 and 1985.

In 1982, the boxer range was supplemented by the R 80 ST and R 80 RT. Featuring all kinds of different equipment, the boxer was rapidly adjusted to various different market requirements throughout this period, boasting various names and model designations in the process. Engines were available with 650, 800 and 1,000cc capacity, and from 1978 to 1985 there was even a machine below 500cc, the R 45, in the boxer range.

On 1 February 1979, an invention was registered at the German Patent Office in München which was subsequently to become the starting point for a new development by BMW sanctioned by the Board only 20 days later. This compact drive system for motorcycles com-

*The 1982-built **R 80 GT** was a road version of the enduro and featured a single rear-wheel swinging arm, the BMW monolever*

prised a water-cooled straight-four power unit which was installed lying down in the motorcycle, with shaft drive and a single swinging arm. This was the birth of the BMW K generation, with an engine that was mounted on only four bolts in the tubular spaceframe.

The 1,000cc machine was followed by its smaller brother, the K 75, in 1985. This served as the entry-level model into the K series and featured a 75bhp 750cc three-cylinder engine.

A further improvement was introduced in 1989, in an even higher-performance version of the K 100; a 100bhp super sports machine that had four-valve technology, Digital Motor Electronics, Paralever swinging arm rear suspension and four-piston brake callipers. It also featured optimised streamlining, with integral front wheel cover; it was called the K 1 in analogy to BMW's M 1 and Z 1 sports cars.

Since 1985, BMW's motorcycle engineers had been working on an anti-lock brake system for their machines. In 1988, this revolutionary technology then entered production; ABS was offered initially for the K 100 models, then also for the K 75 series. Until the very early

Previous pages: main picture *BMW K 1100 RS illustrated with optional ABS;* inset left: *R 1100 RS with R259 engine;* inset right *1993 model BMW K 1*

BMW K 1100 RS

Engine: liquid-cooled four-cylinder inline DOHC
Capacity: 1,092cc
Inlet/outlet diameter: 26.5/23mm (1.03/0.9in)
Output: 74kW (100bhp) at 7,500rpm
Bore and stroke: 70.5 × 70mm (2.75 × 2.73in)
Transmission: five-speed shaft-driven with dry clutch
Brakes: Brembo front 305mm (12in) twin discs; rear 285mm (11.22in) single disc; optional ABS
Tyres: front 120/70 VR 17; rear 160/60 VR 18
Dimensions: length 2,230mm (86.97in); width 800mm (31.2in); wheelbase 1,565mm (61.04in); seat height 800mm (31.2in); weight 268kg (590.94lb); tank 22 litres (4.84 Imp/5.81 US gal)
Performance: top speed over 220km/h (136.62mph)
Electronics: Bosch Motronic ignition/injection; optional three-way catalytic converter
Frame: tubular spaceframe
Suspension: front spring travel 135mm (5.265in); rear Paralever

BMW K 1

Engine: liquid-cooled four-cylinder inline DOHC
Capacity: 987cc
Inlet/outlet diameter: 26.5/23mm (1.03/0.9in)
Output: 74kW (100bhp) at 8,000rpm; maximum torque 100Nm (74ft/lb) at 6,750rpm
Bore and stroke: 67 × 70mm (2.61 × 2.73in)
Transmission: five-speed shaft-driven with single-plate 180mm (7.02in) diameter dry clutch
Brakes: Brembo front 305mm (12in) twin discs; rear 285mm (11.22in) single disc; optional ABS
Tyres: front 120/70 VR 17; rear 160/60 VR 18
Dimensions: length 2,230mm (86.97in); width 760mm (29.64in); wheelbase 1,565mm (61.04in); seat height 780mm (30.42in); weight 259kg (571lb); fuel tank 22 litres (4.84 Imp/5.81 US gal)
Performance: top speed over 230km/h (142.83mph); acceleration 0-100km/h (62mph) in 3.9 seconds
Electronics: Bosch Motronic ignition/injection
Frame: tubular spaceframe, engine loadbearing
Suspension: Marzocchi telescopic front fork; rear BMW Paralever

BMW R 100 GS Paris-Dakar

Engine: oil and air-cooled four-stroke flat twin boxer ohv with two valves per cylinder
Capacity: 980cc
Carburettor: two 40mm (1.56in) Bings
Output: 44kW (60hp) at 6,500rpm; maximum torque 76Nm (56ft/lb) at 3,750rpm
Bore and stroke: 94 × 70.6mm (3.67 × 2.75in)
Brakes: front 285mm (11.12in) single disc; rear 200mm (7.8in) drum
Performance: top speed 180km/h (111.78mph)

Below: *BMW's 1993 model, the R 100 GS Paris-Dakar*

1990s, BMW remained the world's only motorcycle manufacturer able to offer such an outstanding safety feature.

On 18 March 1991, BMW celebrated the production of the millionth BMW motorcycle, a K 75 RT handed over by Eberhard von Kuenheim, Chairman of the Board of BMW AG, for the use of the German Red Cross. This total of one million BMW motorcycles is made up of approximately 230,000 single-cylinder machines, along with 634,000 two-cylinders, 38,000 three-cylinders and some 98,000 four-cylinder models. Total motorcycle sales reached more than 35,000 units worldwide in 1992, the best year for BMW motorbikes.

73

HARLEY-DAVIDSON

In 1903, William (Bill) S Harley and Arthur Davidson joined forces to create one of the most famous names in the biking world. These two next-door neighbours from Milwaukee, Wisconsin, spent their late teens developing small engines as a hobby, one of which powered a rowing boat which Bill used for trout fishing.

During 1900, Harley and Davidson, who were both employed at the Barth Manufacuring company, acquired from workmate Emil Kroeger the blueprints of a small De Dion engine. Kroeger had been employed by the Aster company in Paris, manufacturing the De Dion-Bouton engine, and had taken the blueprints with him when he emigrated to North America.

For the next two years, most evenings were spent by the partners in designing and then building their engine, a 54×73mm ($2\frac{1}{8} \times 2\frac{7}{8}$in) bore and stroke, the intention being that it would provide the propulsion for a heavyweight pedal cycle frame.

Harley and Davidson were now joined part-time by Walter Davidson, Arthur's elder brother. As the project developed, they were forced to move out of the Davidson house into a small basement workshop which was equipped with a lathe, a drill press and a good range of hand tools.

The prototype bike finally emerged in the Spring of 1903, only to prove after testing that the frame was too weak and the engine's power insufficient. Bill designed a new engine with a 76.2×88.9mm ($3 \times 3\frac{1}{2}$in) wide bore and stroke, giving a displacement of 161.29cc (25 cu in). Heavier flywheels and castings were used and a newly-designed frame, complete with a loop in which the engine sat, was built. The first true Harley-Davidson was born, albeit a few years behind the products of their great rivals, Indian, Excelsior and Pope.

A 3×4.5m (10×15ft) workshop was built in the back garden of the Davidson family house at 38th Street, Highland Avenue, complete with lathe, drill press and the words 'Harley Davidson Motor Co' painted over the door.

In the winter months of 1903/4, two machines were built for their purchasers who were required to put up half of the price as a deposit, which was used to finance the building of the bikes which were priced at $200.00.

New orders were soon placed,

and in 1904 Walter became the very first full-time employee, together with four part-time workers who were taken on in enlarged premises. Three further bikes had been completed by the end of 1904, with another five in 1905.

During 1906, with a move to new premises and Arthur finally joining the company full-time, almost one bike per week was produced and this rose to almost three per week in 1907, the same year in which their first orders were received from the police department.

Harley-Davidson now had an established limited dealer network and on 22 September 1907, Harley-Davidson Motor Company of Milwaukee became legally corporate with Walter Davidson its first president and general manager, his brother Arthur general sales manager and company secretary and William Harley chief engineer and designer. The shares were bought by all 17 of the company's employees and then the capital was ploughed back in to finance expansion.

From the outset the Harley-Davidson was fitted with large silencers, the standard colour was switched from black to grey after the first two years of production, and above all they were durable and solidly-built

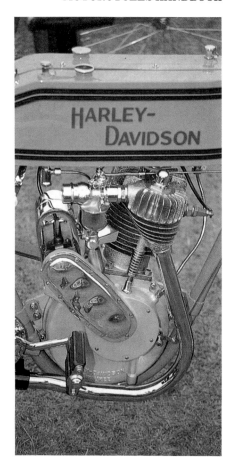

The first full production motorcycle to bear the Harley-Davidson marque

machines. In 1913 the company was able to announce that its first production machine had successfully covered 160,900km (100,000 miles) with no major component having needed to be replaced.

By 1910, production at the Chestnut Street factory had increased to 3,200 bikes per year, including the original 3hp and increased 5hp engines. In 1909 Harley-Davidson had just introduced its second model, the Sixty-one, powered by a 7hp engine capable of a top speed of 97km/h (50mph) of which 27 were built in the year, but it was deemed a failure because the atmospheric intake valve which had worked successfully on the single engine was not suitable for the V-twin engine that Harley-Davidson had been developing. Bill Harley eventually resorted to the use of the mechanical intake valve.

In 1912 Bill Harley fitted a Model X8E with the first properly functioning clutch to be used on a motorcycle; it proved to be a resounding success, and made the machine the most manageable for its day when stop-starting among traffic.

Harley-Davidson's first competitive success came in 1908, when Walter Davidson won the Catskill Mountains of New York Endurance Run, seeing off 64 other competitors entered on 17 different makes of bike. The two-day event covered a gruelling 587km (365 miles), which Walter had completed without needing to resort to spares or repairs.

Bill Ottaway joined Harley-Davidson in 1913, setting up the first race department and developing the twin to produce more power with less vibration. The following year, Harley-Davidson officially entered the race arena and won the Birmingham, Alabama one-hour national championship, which was followed in 1915 by a further 26 major wins.

During the First World War, the Milwaukee production line produced 20,000 model 61J bikes for military action and at the end of the War Harley was able to boast of a 2,000-strong dealer network around the world, which accounted for fully 15% of production. At home, little affected by the European conflict, the Ottaway-led racing division was touring the country, virtually unbeatable on its 11-K racing models powered by the 61 engine, which featured four valves per cylinder and produced 41kW (55hp); it was capable of more than 160km/h (100mph).

In 1919, the W Sport Twin was launched, a flat twin that found no favour with the public, which still preferred the V-twin configuration; but this disappointment did not hold Harley back. Now the factory could employ a workforce of 1,800 and production capacity at its

Above: *the 11-F had the sliding, three-speed transmission lever, sited on the petrol tank*

7,200m^2 (400,000 sq ft) factory was increased to 70,000 bikes per year.

The competition in the early 920s came in the form of Henry Ford, whose black Model T cost 265.00 compared to a Harley 74 which was priced at $325 in 1926. Harley production dropped alarmingly to just 10,000 units. In 1923 the race programme was suspended. Harley survived; others did not, and in 1928 it was able to launch new machines,

the twin-cam JD61 and JDH74; impressive bikes, they both featured front brakes.

Sales picked up in 1929, new bikes were launched and then in the early 1930s the economy slumped. The many American motorcycle factories which, having entered a price-fixing agreement in the 1920s, were out to look after themselves and the actions of Harley-Davidson at this time left a lot to be desired. Even so, its disparate measures at the cruel expense of its rivals still left Harley with its worst year in ten in 1933.

The sales upturn began in 1934, as the world economy bottomed out, the USA emerged from the Depression and the Model 61E Knucklehead got off the drawing board. The first ohv motorcycle to be built in the United States, it had a 1,000cc engine which powered the heavy 272kg (600lb) bike to 145km/h (90mph). At Daytona Beach, Joe Petrali recorded a flying mile averaged at 219km/h (136.18mph) on the 61E.

The UL and ULH models followed, both proving to be highly successful and popular across a wide range of purchasers for their ruggedness and efficiency.

Above: *the Harley Knucklehead motor ushered in overhead valve technology*

During the Second World War, Harley-Davidson produced the models WLA and WLC, of which some 90,000 were produced. The WLC model was built to Canadian government specifications, and supplied to both the Canadian and Allied armies. The WLA combat specification developed by Harley and discussed earlier *page 12–13* included a front fork mounted Thompson SMG holster and ammunition box, rear

Right: *the combat-ready WLA*

leather bags, transmission and engine sump guard, front and rear blackout lamps, oil bath air filter, windshield assembly and leg shields.

At the end of the War effort, Harley was left with enough spares to build a further 30,000 machines. To these must be added around 15,000 Harleys and some 6,000 Indian 741s sold off by the US government onto the civilian market. It helped popularise motorbikes, and for 1948 Harley planned production

A stock Sportster 883 is ready to compete in the Harley-Davidson Twin Sport or 883 Dirt Track series

at 30,000 units per year. Ne models were updates of the (and 74 which were launche without being fully tested an suffered from overheatin problems.

The 125cc 61 or Panhead as later became known, was single-cylinder lightweigh two-stroke which from 194 onwards had hydraulicall damped sprung forks. The 74 wa given the name of Hydra-Glide

By the late 1950s, Harley ha said goodbye to the only othe US motorcycle manufacture left, Indian, and had to itse the big touring bike and polic force markets. In fact, in 196(the Harley range went from th

55cc Taleglide straight up to he 883cc Sportster XL, with othing in between. To fill this laring gap in its range, Harley nerged with the Italian Aer-nacchi company and in 1961 ntroduced the 250cc Sprint, a ike which was capable of a 29km/h (80mph) performance ut it was not a Harley, and fur-hermore it was not a success. 'his was not a big blow to larley, but the invasion of the ser-friendly Japanese bike vas. Harley's share of the US narket dropped to a mere 6% by 965.

Harley's answer was firstly to o public with the company and hen to launch a new machine, which was in effect the 74 Duo Glide with an electric start. The new model was called the Electra Glide, and although upgraded and modified over the years, the Electra Glide was to remain the most sought-after as well as dreamed-about fully dressed-up touring model for the next quarter-century. The most widely known bike throughout the world, it proved to be a milestone at Harley, being powered by the last of its Panhead motors.

Below: *the 1994 Ultra Classic Electra Glide, which features new Electra Glo Light Rails and a rider back rest*

Harley-Davidson FLHS Electra Glide^R Sport

Engine: OHV V^{2R} Evolution^R, vibration isolation mounted
Capacity: 1,340cc
Carburettor: 40mm (1.56in) constant velocity with enricher and accelerator pump
Output: maximum torque 94Nm (69.5ft/lb) at 3,600rpm
Bore and stroke: 88.8 × 108mm (3.463 × 4.212in)
Transmission: five-speed with Gates aramid fibre reinforced Poly Chain^R belt final drive and multi-plate clutch with diaphragm spring in oil bath; double-row chain primary drive
Brakes: front 292 × 5.1mm (11.39 × 0.199in); rear 292 × 7.6mm (11.39 × 0.296in)
Tyres: front MT 90b16; rear MT 0b16
Dimensions: length 2,394mm (93.37in); wheelbase 1,598.7mm (62.35in); clearance 145.2mm (5.66in); seat height 685.8mm (26.75in); weight 317.62kg (700.35lb)
Electronics: V-Fire III$^®$ electronic breakerless ignition with solid-state dual-stage advance

Left: *detail from the 1994 Ultra Classic Electra Glide; the specification above is for the 1993 year model*

Unfortunately the Juneau Avenue factory was poorly-equipped to deal with any sort of boom; Harley was being left behind and by 1967 was on the brink of liquidation, saved by a sell-out to AMF in January 1969. A new advertising programme was launched, calling the bikes the 'All-American Freedom Machine'. Just at the time when the film *Easy Rider* was released, AMF immediately expanded production and model range, opening a new plant at York, Pennsylvania, to capitalise on the new rider-bike association that had been discovered.

In 1971, the FX1200 Super Glide was launched, the first large-capacity Harley to be sold without any of the usual touring bike trappings, but it was not enough. The Harley production line was not efficient, too many bikes left the factory in a faulty condition and the word soon spread. Police department orders were lost, and what made things worse for Harley was the growing success of rivals such as the Honda Goldwing, then being assembled in the United States, and the large Kawasaki 900 and 1,000cc fours.

In 1980 the FLT Tour Glide was launched, a five-gear giant capable of 96km/h (60mph) at just 3,000rpm. The following year AMF, in despair at the continued drain on funds that Harley was proving to be, had engineered a management buyout, returning the company to the bike enthusiast from the giant corporation.

Unfortunately the timing of the buyout coincided with the enormous recession and the dumping of large quantities of Japanese-built bikes onto the market. Harley cut back on production, laying off workers, and by 1982 production was running at just 50%. Harley announced its revised engine in 1983, the new Evolution^R engine which it had begun developing back in 1977 under AMF's direction. A low-tech air-cooled 45° V-twin with push-rod operated overhead valves was designe to conform to the harsher pollution and emission contro laws. The new engine proved to be 15% more powerful, mor fuel-efficient and also totall reliable and was finally introduced through a range of fiv models in 1985.

Citicorp, which had been th main source of finance in th management buyout, asked fo its money back in 1986. Harle, went public, a successful mov that propelled it forward from strength to strength and th Springer Softail was launche in 1988 to mark the company' eighty-fifth anniversary.

Below: *classic Harley; the 1994 FXTS Springer Softail*

HONDA

Soichiro Honda was born in 1906, the eldest son of a blacksmith. He rose from poverty to become a household name, having left school at 16 and learnt the motor trade as an apprentice before opening his own garage at the age of 25. He later went into the manufacturing of piston rings, which proved to be a disaster that nearly bankrupted him.

In an attempt to discover why the piston ring was unsuccessful, he had approached a local university professor who then analysed the metal, diagnosing a lack of silicon, which Honda had never heard of, and so he enrolled at the Hamamatsu Institute of Technology for a metallurgy course. His attendance record was not good, and resulted in his being advised that he would not be awarded a diploma, to which he replied 'The diploma? That's worth less than a cinema ticket. The ticket guarantees you can get into the cinema, but the diploma can't guarantee that you make a living.'

Honda sold his piston-ring company in 1945, and following a year in which he painted the town red, he returned to establish the first Honda Technical Research Institute in 1946. The Institute was a garden shed which measured 5.49×3.66m (18×12ft), and was situated on a levelled bomb site. This was to be where today's motor trade giant had its origins, however, its operation was based on the solution of a simple problem. 'I did not want to ride the incredibly crowded trains and buses myself', said Honda, 'and it became impossible for me to drive my car because of the petrol shortage', so he purchased some surplus military engines, which were then fitted to bicycles. When in the following year the supply of military engines had ran out, Honda designed and built his own, with his 12 employees turning out the first Honda engine, the A-type auxiliary engine. Owing to the lack of petrol, many different fuels were used in the Honda engines, including resin squeezed from pine roots. Honda had bought up some pine forest himself, and formed a fuel from a mixture of pine root resin and petrol purchased on the black market. The Honda nickname for the engine was 'the Chimney'. Postwar Japan suffered from severe petrol shortage, so it is no wonder that these miserly power-assisted bikes were in great demand; so much so, that the following year a second factory was built and then the Honda Technical Research Institute was incorporated into the Honda Motor Company Ltd that September.

Initial capital was 1 million yen, and the first actual motorcycle to bear the Honda name appeared in 1949, the Dream D type. This was a 98cc 2-cycle model that was so popular that Honda's first main sales office was opened in Tokyo in 1950. Honda's phenomenal growth, from nothing to the world's largest motorcycle manufacturer in less than 20 years, was masterminded by Takeo Fujisawa, a marketing and organisational genius who was to provide transportation for people by breaking down all the existing social barriers, fashions and beliefs in order to create a new non-enthusiast market. Fujisawa was made managing director in 1949.

In 1951, a completely new compact 4-cycle engine was developed to power the new Honda Dream E type. The following year, Honda marketed the F Cub, the very first in a line of 50cc engines that were to revolutionise the motorcycle market. With this new engine, Honda began to transform itself into a nationwide marketing force; the popularity of the Honda models led to a further expansion of production capabilities. Two new factories came on line at Shirako and Yamato in 1953, and at Aoi in 1954. The new H type general purpose engine was launched in 1953.

Honda announced his intention to challenge for the famed Isle of Man TT race in 1954, also introducing his first scooter, the 200cc Juno K type, and in the following year launched the Dream SA type and the Bently (Handy). By now, Honda was Japan's leading manufacturer of motorcycles.

In 1957, the Dream C70 250cc 4-cycle touring machine was introduced and in 1958 the Super Cub, a step-through type motorcycle, easy and inexpensive for the average person.

Now Honda's TT challenge was ready, and at his very first attempt in 1959, at this gruelling event, came away with the team award. In 1961, Honda walked off with the top five places in both the 125 and 250cc classes, an added boost for Honda's worldwide expansion programme. The American Honda Motor Co Inc was established in 1959 so as to handle marketing which was based on

Top: *the Dream A type of 1947*

Below: *the Super Cub C 100 of 1958*

a revolutionary new appeal 'You meet the nicest people on a Honda', a campaign that transformed the motorcycle image by making it clear that the motorcycle was not just for the black leather set, but was instead a convenient and also economical style of personal transportation for both business and leisure.

The Suzuka factory started production in 1960, as the world's largest motorcycle plant.

European Honda was formed in 1961, (since renamed Honda Deutschland GmbH) and Honda (Benelux NV) the following year, and immediately began

Above: *Honda 1957 Dream C 70 250cc four-stroke*

manufacture of moped models for the European market. The South-East Asian market was opened up in 1964, with the formation of Asia Honda Motor Co Ltd. For the first time ever, in 1966 a single manufacturer, Honda, won all five solo World Championships in *Grand Prix* races for 50, 125, 250, 350 and 500cc classes. The revolutionary four-cylinder conversion 67hp Honda Dream CB750 Four was launched in 1969, and in 1971 Honda produced its 15 millionth motorcycle, having passed the 10 million mark in

Above: *from 1959, the Honda Dream CB750 Four*

January 1968.

As Honda celebrated its twenty-fifth anniversary in 1973, Soichiro Honda and Takeo Fujisawa stepped down from office to take lifetime Supreme Advisor positions, and the presidency passed to Kiyoshi Kawashima, who had joined the tiny engine shop in 1947 as an engineer.

In 1976, Honda introduced the 50cc Road Pal (Honda Express for export) series of 'family bikes' which were to prove the most rapidly expanding section of the market for the rest of the decade.

The Honda Endurance Racing Team won the European Endurance Race at Barcelona in 1979, and the following year saw the start of production of the CX500 Turbo, the world's first turbocharged mass production motorcycle, which was produced at Honda's Hamamatsu factory in 1981.

The VF400 and VF750 series were launched in 1982, and in 1985 Freddie Spencer completed a unique double for Honda when he took both the 250 and 500cc GP Road Racing titles, while David Thorpe captured the 500cc Motocross title and Gerard Couldray and Patric

Igoa extended their joint reign as World Endurance Champions.

Honda announced in 1987 that it would introduce an anti-lock braking system for motorcycles in 1989. At the same time, it announced the first speed-controlled electric reversing system for a motorcycle in the Gold Wing GL1500. This had a horizontally-opposed 1,500cc six-cylinder engine, which was the largest ever produced by Honda. Brand new generation CBR1000 and CBR600s went on sale, together with the Transalp 600V which introduced a new concept of touring. Later the International Motorcycle Show in Birmingham, England, launched the VFR750R and NTV600 motorcycles by Honda, and Wayne Gardner won the World 500cc Road Race series with Honda, also securing the 250cc series along with the world 500cc and 250cc motocross titles.

Honda's commitment to race motorcycles is the foundation upon which the company's commercial success has been based. In road racing, Honda has won more than 30 World Championships with literally dozens of *Grand Prix* victories. Honda has won world titles at 50, 125, 250, 350, and 500cc GPs. Joey Dunlop was five times TT

Honda's state-of-the-art ST 1100 Pan-European ABS/TCS (E type

Formula 1 World Champion and in 1988 Fred Merkel won the first World Superbike Championship. Honda's success also extends to winning the toughest series of all, the World 24-hour Endurance Championship. In recent years, Freddie Spencer won Honda's first 500cc World Championship in 1983 and then took the unique 250cc and 500cc double in 1985.

After racing for Honda UK Australian Wayne Gardner was runner-up in the 1986 500cc World Championship and took the title in 1987. West German Toni Mang won the 250cc Championship in the same year, and in 1988 Spaniard Sito Pons was World Champion, also at 250cc.

Honda's off-road competition machines have also enjoyed world championship success. The multi-British Champion Dave Thorpe won the 500cc Motocross title in 1985 and 1986 and Georges Jobe was World Champion in 1987. Eric Geboers, the only man to win world titles in all three solo motocross classes, took the 250cc Championship in 1987 and the 500cc in 1988, when Jean-Michel Bayle also gave Honda its first 125cc World title.

Honda ST 1100 Pan-European ABS/TCS (E type)

Country of origin: Japan
Engine: four-stroke liquid-cooled 90° V4 DOHC
Capacity: 1,084cc
Carburettor: four 31.4mm (1.22in) CV type
Output: 74kW (100bhp) at 7,500rpm; maximum torque 113Nm (83.6ft/lb) at 6,000rpm
Bore and stroke: 73 × 64.8mm (2.85 × 2.53in)
Transmission: five-speed enclosed shaft-driven
Brakes: front 316mm (12.32in) twin discs with ABS; rear 316mm (12.32in) disc with ABS

Tyres: front 110/80 V18; rear 160/70 V17
Dimensions: length 2,285mm (89.12in); width 935mm (36.47in) with panniers; wheelbase 1,555mm (60.65in); clearance 145mm (5.66in); seat height 800mm (31.2in); weight 293kg (646lb); fuel tank 28 litres (6.16 Imp/7.4 US gal)
Electronics: computer-controlled
Frame: steel double cradle
Suspension: 41mm (1.6in) cartridge type front fork with Torque Reactive Anti-dive Control (TRAC); rear single-side conventional damper

TRIUMPH

Triumph is a true British bike with today's range conceived, designed, developed and manufactured in Leicestershire, in a new purpose-built factory. The current range of six models is based on a modular philosophy, sharing many key components, thus providing easier and quicker maintenance.

Today's engines are all liquid cooled dohc inlines with three or four cylinders, unlike the classic design of the vertical twin engine layout introduced in 1938 and with which the name of Triumph had become synonymous. The first such engine layout appeared in the 198cc Speed Twin, a forerunner of the larger and more renowned Thunderbird, which was to be launched in 1949. This was a 649cc tourer that produced 34bhp at 6,000rpm and had a top speed in excess of 162km/h (100mph). Triumph did not switch from the vertical twin layout until the 1960s, when it introduced the transverse three-cylinder Trident, which had a 740cc ohv engine with a 67×70mm (2.61×2.3in) bore and stroke, and a top speed of 200km/h (125mph).

Illustrated left is the Daytona 900, powered by an 885cc three-cylinder engine.

INDEX

The Moto Guzzi Nevada 750 is illustrated to demonstrate the calculations of various measurements

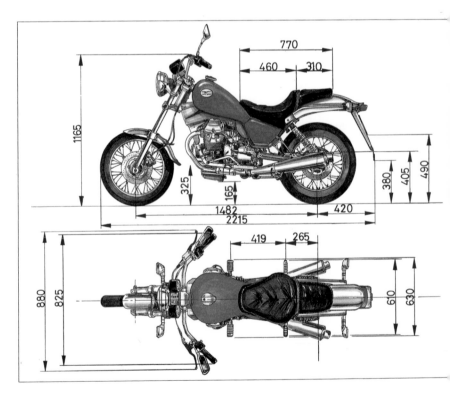